D0237226

ONE WEEK LOAN

75 WAYS TO LIVEN UP YOUR TRAINING

A collection of energizing activities

75 Ways to Liven Up Your Training

A collection of energizing activities

MARTIN ORRIDGE

Illustrated by Simon Jarvis

Gower

658.3124
ORR

© Martin Orridge 1996

All rights reserved. No part of this publication may be reproduced, stored in a retrieval system, or transmitted in any form or by any means, electronic, mechanical, photocopying, recording or otherwise without the permission of the publisher.

Published by
Gower Publishing Limited
Gower House
Croft Road
Aldershot
Hampshire GU11 3HR
England

Gower
Old Post Road
Brookfield
Vermont 05036
USA

1146765-7

Learning Resources
Centre

Reprinted 1997

Martin Orridge has asserted his right under the Copyright, Designs and Patents Act 1988 to be identified as the author of this work.

British Library Cataloguing in Publication Data
Orridge, Martin
    75 ways to liven up your training
    1. Work groups   2. Employees – Training of
    I. Title   II. Seventy-five ways to liven up your training
    658.3'124'04

ISBN 0 566 07774 4

Library of Congress Cataloging-in-Publication Data
Orridge, Martin, 1947–
    75 ways to liven up your training : a collection of energizing activities /
    Martin Orridge : illustrated by Simon Jarvis.
        p. cm.
        ISBN 0-566-07774-4
        1. Employees—Training of—Problems, exercises, etc.   I. Title
    HF5549.5.T7077   1996
    658.3' 124—dc20
                                                                    96-8092
                                                                    CIP

Typeset in Palatino by Manton Typesetters, 5–7 Eastfield Road, Louth, Lincolnshire, LN11 7AJ, UK and printed in Great Britain at the University Press, Cambridge.

This book is dedicated to everyone who develops people,
from the play school to the senior executive programmes.
We have so very much in common.

Contents

Preface

Some years ago, before I became involved in people development, I was asked to give two presentations at a management training course. I arrived at the hotel during coffee time as I was scheduled to run my two, rather heavy, sessions on either side of lunch. It was a glorious June day and, even with my untrained eye, I could see that the participants were restless. By the time I came to start my first presentation the temperature was in the 80s Fahrenheit, and it continued climbing during the hour until lunch. I felt that the members of the group were, out of politeness to a visitor, trying to participate, but it was becoming a lost cause.

To compound the problem the hotel had put on a sumptuous lunch with plenty of alcohol, and it was quite apparent that the delegates had little chance of concentrating after lunch. I pondered how I might rescue the situation and concluded that I had to scrap my presentation and replace it with something energetic and creatively stimulating. Having skipped desert and coffee I scoured the hotel for inspiration and resources. Within half an hour I had gathered together paper, card, adhesive tape, bricks and so on and an outline plan for an exercise. On the participants' return they were organized into three groups, with two groups being asked to build towers to a particular specification and the third team acting as their consultants. The participants became reenergized and as time progressed, if the session started to flag, I threw in a few changes to bring it back to life again. The exercise had saved me from creeping death, and in the review session I even managed to cover most of the points I had in my presentation, but so much more powerfully.

Some months later I took the opportunity to become much more closely involved in people development. Whilst in that role I developed more interventions and also exchanged them with friends and colleagues. This book contains 75 of my favourites. They cover a number of situations, from 'ice breaking' when opening an event through to 'closing off' at the end. The origin of many have been lost in time. For example, I first remember playing Frisbee golf in the 1950s using enamel plates, long before plastic Frisbees arrived. Many of the exercises were first made up on the spur of the moment to deal with a crisis. They were then refined and became well loved standards. Over the years I have shared thoughts and ideas with many people development professionals, and in particular I would like to mention Jo Anne Freeman, Chris Lever and Ioan Tenner who were instrumental in my becoming involved in this area myself.

If you are at all like me you will use the exercises in this book as a basis on which to develop your own particular brand of exercise. I wish you every success in developing your people.

Martin Orridge

Introduction

To help you select the appropriate event, the exercises in this book are grouped according to type or function. Within each exercise, the material is presented in a standard sequence: a description of the exercise, an explanation of its purpose, a list of the materials required, the approximate duration of the exercise, details of the procedure, review suggestions, and some variations on the theme. This information will be of use during the planning and execution phases.

An explanation of each element is given below:

Description   This is a brief overview of what happens during the exercise.

Purpose   This section explains the reason for the exercise. For example, the purpose may be to develop a skill or just get people working with each other.

Materials   A list of what you need to run the exercise is given here. The requirements are sometimes very specific. At other times, it is up to the trainer to choose a set of materials, and the choice will depend on what is available. I often just look around and see what resources are close to hand. Just changing some of the materials can give a new edge to an exercise you have used a number of times.

Duration   Approximate timings are given for each exercise. These average figures can easily fluctuate by 50% either way. Human beings are not machines, and they can be very unpredictable. I once lost almost an hour during an important role play when my cotrainer, who was supposed to start the exercise, fell asleep in his room. The participants thought that his non-appearance was an initiative exercise, and had a great deal of fun attempting to work out how the exercise should start. My watchword is 'do not be ruled by the clock'. Always be prepared for the unexpected, and try to use it to your advantage.

Procedure   This section is a step by step guide to running the exercise. Do not just read out the steps to the participants. Make notes, and then add your own flavour to the exercise. Better still, extend the exercise, and make it your own.

Review   A review of the exercise is optional. Sometimes, a group discussion is just not appropriate, particularly if the participants have been under a great deal of stress, and the team members need to discuss what has happened amongst themselves. This section gives some pointers as to the types of discussion you could lead. However, the participants are human beings, and they may have learnt something that is quite different from what you expected. Be flexible, and there should be no problems.

Variations   Options for modifications to the exercise are listed here.

I

Ice breakers

I once had a conversation with a nephew of mine. He said 'why did the 10 ton elephant walk on the frozen pond?'. 'I don't know – why did the elephant walk on the frozen pond?' I responded. 'I don't know either', replied my nephew, 'but it makes a good ice breaker'.

A good ice breaker can get your event off to a high energy start, as opposed to creeping death whilst each participant does his or her 2 minute introduction.

I have included 15 ice breaking exercises in this book. Most of these, and in particular **Birthdays**, **Name Game**, **First Impression Fantasy** and **Stick 'Em Up**, can be used at any time during an event to re-energize the participants.

Ice breakers can be used with small and large groups, but their effectiveness is decreased if there are fewer than six participants. I would not use **Cocktail Party**, **Stick 'Em Up** or **Birthdays** when there were fewer than ten participants; the dynamics would not be right.

The start of an event can set the tone for the next few days, and so you should always be ready to step in during an ice breaking exercise if energy is beginning to flag or creeping death sets in.

1   Birthdays

Description   The participants have to form themselves into a line in order of the day and month of their birthdays.

Purpose   The exercise develops group cooperation and problem solving skills, and it helps the participants to get to know each other. It is also a good energizer.

Materials   None.

Timing   5 minutes.

Procedure
1. Explain that the objective is for the participants to form a line in order of the day and month of their birthdays (1 January to 31 December order). If two or more people have the same birthday, they arrange themselves in alphabetical order of surname (and first name if necessary).
2. Participants then rise to their feet and walk around. When they meet another participant they exchange names and birthdays.

3. When the line has been formed, each participant in the row calls out his or her name and birthday so that you can check that the objective has been achieved.

Review Review the group's success at problem solving, if this is necessary.

Variations 1. Sort by first names in alphabetical order.
2. Blindfold the participants.

2   Cinderella

Description   The participants find their partners by fitting their right shoe.

Purpose   This is an ice breaking exercise for when you want to pair up the participants, for example for the paired exercises, **Pictorial Interview**, or **First Impression Fantasy**.

Materials   A large box, bag or sack.

Duration   5 minutes.

Procedure
1. Half of the participants take off their right shoes and place them in the box.
2. The other half of the participants pick a shoe at random.
3. They then attempt to find their Cinderella by exchanging names with each of the participants without a shoe, and seeing if their shoe fits that person.
4. When the participants have been paired up, they stay in those pairs for whatever is planned next.

Review   None.

Variation   Use other suitable personal items, such as keys and business cards, if shoes are felt to be inappropriate. For example, old photographs can be amusing, but this needs to be organized before the event.

3   Cocktail Party

Description   The participants gather together as if at a cocktail party. They mingle and exchange small talk whilst giving some key facts about themselves. When the 'party' is over, the participants discuss what they have found out about each other.

Purpose   This exercise encourages the participants to mix and get to know each other. It tests their information gathering and retention skills, and demonstrates the strength of first impressions.

Materials   A flip chart for capturing personal data (optional).
Coffee or glasses or cups for each participant (optional).

Timing   30 minutes, depending on the number of participants.

Procedure   1. Explain that this is an ice breaking exercise. Then explain that the participants are going to attend a cocktail party.
2. Give the participants 2 minutes to think of three truths about themselves in addition to their name and occupation, for example 'I am married, drive a Ferrari, and enjoy photography'.
3. The participants circulate at the 'cocktail party'. They engage in polite conversation, and tell each other their names, occupations, and the three true things about themselves. The participants are encouraged not to blurt out their truths and then rush on to the next conversation.
4. Allow about 10 minutes, depending on the number of participants, for each person to have at least four conversations. Then ask everyone to return to his or her seat.
5. Select participants one at a time, and ask the group what they know about the person.
6. If you want to, capture the data on a flip chart.

Review   Lead a brief discussion about business and social gatherings. Discuss the techniques that each participant used to remember key facts about the others.

Examine first impressions and personal impact. Ask each participant to think about what people remember about him or her after a first meeting. These thoughts should not be shared at the start of the course.

Variations   None.

4   First Impression Fantasy

Description   Paired participants who have little or no knowledge of each other describe what they believe the other was like when they were 15 years old.

Purpose   This is a small group ice breaker that is an opportunity to demonstrate both the power and risk of people using their intuition. This exercise can be used at any time as an amusing energizer.

Materials   None.

Duration   2 minutes for the introduction, and 6 minutes for each pair of interviews.

Procedure
1. Pair off the participants. The pairs exchange names and decide who will go first.
2. One tells the other what he or she believes the other was like at 15. He or she begins the 2 minute monologue with the words 'although I have only just met you, my intuition tells me that at 15 you were…'.
3. At the end of each monologue, the subject gives the speaker a percentage mark for his or her accuracy, and highlights the correct and incorrect points.
4. This exercise can be repeated for all the pairs who have not met before, although about three sessions is probably enough.

Review   The accuracies will probably be in the range 10–80%. Discuss the power of using intuition, and the care that must be taken in exercising it. Finally, remind participants that when they use intuition in the workplace, they must make it clear that this is what they are doing.

Variations   None.

5   Intro Bingo

Description   The participants have to match other participants to a series of facts and record their names in the spaces on a 'bingo card'.

Purpose   This is an energizing ice breaker that ensures that most, if not all, of the participants introduce themselves to the others.

Materials   Prepare a set of bingo sheets. An example of a bingo sheet is shown opposite. The number of questions should be equal to the number of participants, up to a maximum of 16 questions. You also need a pen or pencil for each participant.

Duration   10–15 minutes. This is very dependent on the size of the group.

Procedure
1.   Explain that each participant will be given a bingo sheet. They must then try to achieve a 'full house' by filling in all the blanks on the sheet.
2.   Participants then ask the others questions. They fill in a blank on the bingo sheet by finding someone who matches one of the attributes on the sheet, and recording his or her name on the sheet. Each name can only be written on the sheet once.
3.   When the first participant completes his or her sheet, he or she shouts 'bingo'. The correctness of the sheet is then checked, which introduces/reintroduces many of the participants.

Review   None.

Variations   None.

Example Bingo sheet

Find people who do the following:

1. Plays a musical instrument	2. Shops at Tesco	3. Has worked for the government	4. Has been to France
5. Can whistle [check]	6. Can say a sentence in a language other than English	7. Grows vegetables	8. Exercises regularly
9. Has a hobby which no-one else in the room has	10. Owns a car that is more than three years old	11. Plays golf	12. Has read more than ten Shakespeare plays
13. Likes real ale	14. Owns a cat	15. Is a vegetarian	16. Has bought a Beatles record

Please write the names of the people in the appropriate spaces below. You may only use a name once.

1.	2.	3.	4.
5.	6.	7.	8.
9.	10.	11.	12.
13.	14.	15.	16.

6 Jigsaw

Description   Each participant selects a piece of a jigsaw puzzle. He or she then has to find the other people who hold parts of that puzzle.

Purpose   This exercise is a way of randomly selecting teams from a large group.

Materials   A sheet of thin card or paper for each of the teams (all the sheets should be the same shape and colour).
A pair of scissors.
A pen or pencil for each participant.
A box or bag.
A marker pen (optional).

Duration   5–10 minutes.

Procedure
1. Take some sheets of card or paper (which should all be the same size and colour). There should be one sheet for each of the teams that you are going to form.
2. Cut each sheet into irregular, jigsaw type pieces. For each team's sheet, the number of pieces must equal the number of participants that you are going to allocate to that team. Make sure that you do not duplicate any of the shapes.
3. Put all the pieces of all the sheets into a box or bag, and ask each participant to take a piece. Ask them to write their name on their piece.
4. Explain that there are n separate jigsaw puzzles (where n is the number of teams), and ask them to complete the puzzles. Then take the groups of pieces, note the names, and tell each participant the name of the team to which he or she has been allocated.
5. When all the puzzles have been completed tell the participants that they are now teamed with whoever else supplied pieces to complete the jigsaw. Their names are on the jigsaw pieces.

Review   Lead a discussion about working in groups and simple puzzle solving.

Variation   If you have decided upon team names before the event write the name on each sheet before cutting them into jigsaw pieces. The names will be revealed again when the jigsaws are completed.

7 Name Game

Description The participants form a circle, and throw a ball around. As the ball is thrown by one participant to another, the thrower must call out the catcher's name.

Purpose This exercises helps each participant to remember the names of the others.

Materials Two soft balls are required. I have also used flip chart pens, large rubbers and so on.

Duration 10 minutes.

Procedure 1. Form the participants into a circle, with them facing towards the centre.

2. Each person gives his or her name.
3. Start the exercise with one ball. Select a person in the circle and, as you throw the ball to him or her, call out his or her first name.
4. If you called the correct name, the catcher throws the ball to another person and calls out his or her name. If you called an incorrect name, the catcher calls out his or her own name before throwing the ball to another person.
5. Start the exercise slowly and then gradually increase the tempo. After everybody has had a few turns, stop the exercise and restart it with two balls.
6. Stop when the novelty starts to wear off.

Review   Discuss the need to remember people's names as quickly as possible. Find out the strategies that delegates use for remembering names.

Variations   None. However, it is often a good idea to use this exercise at the start of the second day to see how well delegates are getting to know each other.

8   Pictorial Interview

Description   The participants are paired off. One of each pair interviews the other so that they are able to introduce or present each other to the main group. A flip chart is then prepared to assist with the presentation. Presentations are made to the main group in a variety of styles.

Purpose   This exercise helps pairs of participants to get to know each other. It ensures that everybody is introduced to the group, and allows the participants to practice data collection, organization and presentation techniques.

Materials   A piece of flip chart paper and a flip chart pen for each of the participants.
A pen and paper for each participant to take notes.

Duration   30 or more minutes, depending on the size of the group.

Procedure
1. Pair off the participants, for example to the person he or she is sitting next to.
2. Explain the process.
3. One of each pair interviews the other, and then the interviewee interviews the interviewer. Interviews should last for no more than 5 minutes. Notes may be taken.
4. Having completed the interviews the interviewers have 5 minutes to draw a picture of their interviewee or write down bulleted points about him or her on flip chart paper.
5. Each person is presented by his or her interviewer to the group in a style of the interviewer's choice, for example 'newscaster', 'gameshow host', or 'sports commentator'. Each presentation should take a maximum of 2 minutes.
6. Hang the flip chart sheets on the wall.

Review   Discussions can cover interviewing techniques, presentations and the use of visual aids.

Variation   After the interview phase, the participants draw their interview style from a container. Allow an extra 5 minutes for the picking of the interview style and the extra preparation needed.

9   Sentenced

Description   The participants describe themselves in one sentence of no more than 30 words.

Purpose   The participants have to decide what the key to their make up is.

Materials   A pen for each participant.
Paper for each participant.

Duration   10 minutes, including 7 minutes to write the sentences.

Procedure   1.   Ask each participant to write a sentence of no more than 30 words that describes him or her.
     2.   When all the sentences have been written, each person reads his or her sentence out to the rest of the group.

Review   Determine how the participants decided what aspect of their characters was really important.

Variations   None.

10 Sell Yourself

Description The members of newly formed teams prepare and deliver brief presentations which describe their combined skills, knowledge and experience.

Purpose This an exercise in team formation. Data handling, facilitation and presentation skills need to be employed for a successful outcome.

Materials A flip chart or an overhead projector and appropriate pens for each team.
Separate breakout rooms, if possible.

Duration 45 minutes for four teams. Add 5 minutes for each additional team.

Procedure
1. Tell the teams that they are forming themselves into a number of new start up companies. The type of business often depends on the membership of the team. Consulting always seems to produce a good result.
2. The teams are given 25 minutes to complete the task.
3. The members of each team need to determine what their combined skills, knowledge and experience and what type of business, service or consultancy they will offer based on these skills, knowledge or experience. Encourage them to look beyond their immediate business skills. I have found that some very interesting ideas emerge from hobbies and other non day to day business skills.
4. When they have determined their skills, and so on, and decided on the services to be offered, each team selects a presenter and prepares a 3–5 minute introductory presentation as if it were the lead in to a major presentation.
5. Each team makes its presentation to the group.

Review Discussions can cover team forming and roles, how the task was carried out, and the many skills that every person possesses that are often forgotten or ignored.

Variations None.

11   Shields

Description   The participants design a heraldic shield that describes themselves and their interests.

Purpose   This approach to group introductions is an alternative to creeping death around the group. It shows the power of visual aids and acts as a prop to participants as they talk.

Materials   A sheet of flip chart paper for each participant.
Flip chart coloured pens for each participant.

Timing   About 30 minutes, depending on number of participants.

Procedure
1. Ask each participant to design a shield and a motto to depict himself or herself. The shield should be divided into quadrants with something different about the participant in each one. Allow 10–15 minutes for drawing the shield.
2. Ask each participant to introduce himself or herself using the shield as a visual aid.
3. Hang the shields on the wall.

Review   Discuss the role of visual aids in presentations.

Variation   Each participant designs a flag or standard to depict himself or herself.

12   Stick 'Em Up

Description   The participants are Wild West gunfighters. When they meet another participant, they see who can draw his or her gun first.

Purpose   This is an ice breaker and ongoing energizer.

Materials   None.

Duration   5 minutes.

Procedure   1.   Explain that every participant is a Wild West gunfighter with two guns.

2. All the participants rise to their feet and walk around the room as if they are going to draw their guns.

3. When two people come face to face, they stop and exchange names in a suitable Western fashion, saying, for example, 'howdy partner, I'm John Smith'.

4. The pair are now in the 'stand off' position. They stare each other out until one of them reaches for his or her guns. When someone uses his or her guns, he or she points two fingers of each hand, like a pair of pistols, at the other person.

5. When this happens, the other person must *not* reach for his or her guns, but instead quickly raise his or her hands in surrender. If he or she should also reach for his or her guns after the partner has drawn, he or she will have been shot and lost the gunfight.

6. After the gunfight, the participants move off to find another gunslinger.

7. *Cautionary note*: This exercise is likely to continue throughout the week and beyond, in bars, supermarkets and so on.

Review   Not necessary.

Variation   When they are in the stand off position, the participants may either reach for their guns or 'stick their hands up', with the objective of getting the other person to copy their action. If the other person does, he or she has lost.

13 Suited

Description   Each participant is dealt a card. He or she then teams up with the other participants who have the same suit. The newly formed team has to perform a simple creative exercise by deciding on a team slogan that incorporates its suit.

Purpose   This is an ice breaker and random teams former with a creative twist.

Materials   A pack of cards, or two or more packs of cards with different backs if there are more than four teams.
Flip chart paper and a pen for each team (optional).

Duration   10 minutes.

Procedure
1. Presort the cards to ensure that you have enough packs for the number of teams, and enough cards in each suit for the numbers in each team.
2. Shuffle the presorted cards and deal one card to each participant. Explain that each participant has to find the other people who have his or her suit. The team then has to devise a slogan which incorporates the name of the suit.
3. The team can then write its slogan on a flip chart and hang it by its team area (optional).

Review   None.

Variation   A card is sent to each participant with his or her joining instructions. Ask the participant to bring the card to the course, and to find the other people with his or her suit during the coffee break before the event starts.

14   What Are We?

Description   A large group is formed into teams by each participant finding the others who belong in the same team.

Purpose   This is an ice breaker and team forming exercise.

Materials   Prepare sets of cards or pieces of paper by writing the names of items on them. There should be a card for every participant.

Duration   5 minutes.

Procedure
1.   In advance of the event, prepare sets of cards or pieces of paper. There should be one set of cards for each team. The number of cards in each set should equal the number of participants to be allocated to that team. Write the names of sets of items on your sets of cards.
2.   An encyclopaedia is a good source of ideas for sets of items. For example, you could have (a) an engine set: piston, crankshaft, bearing, push rod, sump, rocker, (b) an arm and hand bones set: scapula, humerus, radius, ulna, carpus, metacarpus, (c) a sailing boat set: bow, rudder, keel, hull, centreboard, sheet, (d) a Greek amphitheatre set: episcenium, logum, proscenium, thymele, auditorium, orchestra, or (e) a castle set: keep, motte, turret, barbican, moat, portcullis. The degrees of difficulty and ambiguity of the words in the sets should match the participants' level of knowledge of the areas.
3.   Each participant selects one of the folded cards but does not look at it. When all the participants have a card, explain that they must find the other participants with words from the same set on their cards.
4.   When one participant meets another, he or she should exchange information by shaking hands and saying 'I am X [for example "John Smith"] the Y [for example the "rudder"]'. If the two participants believe that they belong together, they should pair up and look for other members of their team until they have found them all.
5.   When all the teams have been formed, check what set of items (for example an 'engine' set) they believe they belong to. This is their team for the event.

Review   None, as this is a team forming ice breaker.

Variation   It can make it more interesting if you introduce some ambiguity, so that an item may belong to more than one set. For example, 'rudder' might belong to a 'boat' set or an 'aeroplane' set.

15 Wishes

Description   Each participant has three wishes about what he or she would like to achieve during the event.

Purpose   This is an icebreaking exercise that collects the participants' expectations of the event.

Materials   A flip chart and pen.
A pencil for each participant.
Paper for each participant.

Duration   45 minutes.

Procedure
1. Allow the participants 5 minutes to think about what they would like to get out of the event, and to decide on one important fact about themselves (or, better still, ask them to think about this before the event).
2. The participants write their wishes down.
3. Each participant give his or her name, the important fact about himself or herself, and the three wishes. The course leader captures these on the flip chart.
4. When all the participants have stated their wishes, the course leader reviews the wishes on the flip chart as honestly as possible whilst giving an overview of the event.

Review   Not applicable.

Variations
1. The participants write their wishes on Post-it®, or similar repositionable notes and stick them on a board or wall so that similar ones can be grouped together.
2. If the group has more than 12 members, break it up into two or more smaller teams. Each team does the exercise, and a team spokesperson reports back the team's main wishes.

II

Team working

Team working is a fact of life in today's organizations, and a great deal of emphasis is placed on being a team player etc. I feel that it has always been necessary to work in teams, and that this was of core importance in humans becoming Earth's current dominant species. For a few decades of this century the harnessing of technology seemed to obscure people's need to work in teams. After that era, the error of our ways became apparent and team working has once again returned to near the top of the training and development agenda.

The exercises in this chapter generally work well with teams of 4–6 people. With teams of fewer than four there is little opportunity for team dynamics to come into play, and more than six introduces the 'too many cooks spoil the broth' effect. Most of the exercises have an element of interteam competition. This need not always be the case.

On occasions I have videotaped the exercises and used them both for group reviews and as an evening resource for teams to review by themselves. Do not videotape a group without first discussing it with them. Some years ago, when I was a course participant, an event came to an abrupt stop for an hour when one participant objected to the sudden appearance of the camera. When we understood the background of the country he came from, we appreciated his concerns. The main worry of participants is usually that the tape might be seen by their manager and put them in a bad light. Erase any tapes yourself at the end of the event.

Sometimes, intergroup competition, particularly when a prize is involved, can result in everybody losing (or no-one winning). This outcome can produce very useful discussions about cooperation and competition. However, you can often ensure a winning outcome if, in the event of no team winning, the 'prize' is awarded to the trainer. I have only received a prize once when this rule has applied. However, even this system can backfire if the teams decide they will not even try.

All outcomes are valuable discussion material. If you know your participants, you will know when to push them and when to ease off.

16   A Better Mousetrap

Description   Teams design and build an innovative or 'crazy' mousetrap.

Purpose   This is a team working and creative exercise.

Materials   A sugar mouse (for the course leader).
Give each team the following:
Paper and pencils or pens for the design phase.
A Meccano® or similar construction set and/or the following:
Plastic bottles.
Ice cream or margarine-type containers.
String.
Adhesive tape.
Card.
Short lengths of wood.
A sugar mouse.

Duration   1.5 hours.

Procedure
1. Allocate the materials. Tell the teams that they are required to design and build a better mousetrap in 75 minutes. Explain that you are looking for new and original ways of dealing with the rodent.
2. After the 75 minutes, the traps are tested with the leader's sugar mouse.

Review   Discuss team working and particularly how the design and construction phases were conducted. Were trial and error methods used, or was time spent on thinking about the requirements and were some tentative designs proposed?

Variation   Award points for the most effective trap and the craziest trap.

17   Crystal Clear

Description   Teams have to separate crystals of salt from sand.

Purpose   This is a creative team exercise.

Materials   For each team a 2 pint (or 1 litre) plastic bottle half filled with a mixture of dry sharp sand and dishwasher salt crystals (use a ratio of sharp sand to salt of about 20:1).
An empty 3.5 pint (or 2 litre) plastic bottle.
Two sheets of flip chart paper.
Adhesive tape.
A ruler.
A pencil.
A pair of scissors.
Ten paper clips (optional).
Plastic re-usable adhesive (optional).
A stapler (optional).

Duration   45 minutes.

Procedure
1. Tell the teams that they have 45 minutes to separate the large crystalline impurities from the sand. The sand must be in one bottle, and the impurities in the other.
2. The winning team is the one that separates the most crystals from the sand.

Review   Examine the various ways in which the teams approached the problem, and how the members of each team arrived at their agreed method. *Note:* There are a number of ways to solve this problem, for example by (a) making a funnel and sieve, (b) constructing a centrifuge (more difficult), (c) spreading the mixture out thinly and picking the crystals out (time consuming), or (d) transferring the mixture to the 3.5 pint (or 2 litre) bottle, adding about 1 pint (or 0.5 litres) of water to the mixture, dissolving the crystals, and pouring the solution off into the 2 pint (or 1 litre) bottle.

Variations   None.

18 Fire Extinguisher

Description   Teams must design and build an implement that they can use to extinguish a candle remotely from 6 feet (or 2 metres).

Purpose   This is a creative team exercise. There are a number of solutions; one is very quick and easy.

Materials   Give each team the following:
One sheet of flip chart paper.
A small piece of candle.
Some matches.
Ten paper clips.
Two elastic bands.
A piece of string with a maximum length of 1 foot (or 0.3 metres).
A piece of adhesive tape with a maximum length of 1 foot (or 0.3 metres).
A piece of re-usable plastic adhesive.
Some tin foil or eight metal foil milk bottle tops.
Note: The candle can be extinguished by making a long cone from the flip chart paper and blowing down the wide end. For the exercise to work, you need to give the teams many other materials such as those listed above. In case none of the teams propose the cone solution, make sure that you are able to make a long cone and blow out the candle.

Duration   10 or more minutes, depending on number of teams.

Procedure   1.   Issue the materials and tell the teams that they have 7 minutes to design and build a candle snuffer to extinguish a candle remotely from 6 feet (or 2 metres). The candle must be extinguished within 15 seconds of the leader saying 'fire'.
2.   *Note:* You must use the words 'candle snuffer' and 'extinguish.' If possible, write the problem statement on a flip chart to reinforce the words.
3.   Whilst the teams are building the snuffers, set up a candle about 2 feet (or 0.6 metres) above the floor, and mark a line 6 feet (or 2 metres) away.
4.   After 7 minutes, each team has 15 seconds to attempt to extinguish the candle using their candle snuffers. The leader starts each team off by saying 'fire.'

Review   If none of the teams use a cone, you may demonstrate the making of a cone and blow out the candle. Start by discussing how each team chose their design. Then consider how the language used in defining a problem can influence the proposed solutions. Finally, examine how the wide range of resources influenced the design.

Variations   None.

19 Grab It

Description   Team members make a device to 'grab' and retrieve a remote object.

Purpose   This is a small group creative problem solving exercise

Materials   String to mark out a 'no-go' zone.
At least one 2 pint (or 1 litre) plastic bottle filled with water or sand for each team.
Give each team the following:
At least two, and preferably more, 5 feet (or 1.5 metres) bamboo canes.
A 3 feet (or 1 metre) length of parcel string.
Adhesive tape.
Ten elastic bands.
20 paper clips.
A pair of scissors.
Any other construction materials that you want to add.

Duration   3–10 minutes.

Procedure   1.   Issue all the team materials.
2.   Place the bottles together on the floor. Mark out a no-go zone with a radius of 6 feet (or 2 metres) around the bottles, or use four chairs to form a square the edge of which is 6 feet (or 2 metres) away from the bottles.
3.   Tell the teams that they have ten minutes to retrieve as many bottles as possible using the materials provided. They will gain 10 points for every bottle retrieved and lose 20 points for every bottle dropped. (You might want to add that the contents are radioactive.) The participants must not enter the no-go zone.

Review   This exercise can be completed successfully by one person using just two canes, a short length of string, and some adhesive tape to provide a fulcrum point. (The canes form a pair of scissors, and the string is tied between the ends of the canes so that it can be looped over the bottle.) With three or more people in a team, a wide range of materials, and competition, all sorts of interesting dynamics come into play. Start by discussing how the teams approached the problem and then examine the dynamics.

Variation   Introduce larger distances and heavier objects as follow-on exercises.

20 Invent a Game

Description   Each team must invent a small or large group exercise or game.

Purpose   This is a creative teamwork exercise which requires the development of unambiguous rules and procedures.

Materials   As much or as little as each team requires (the course leader defines these boundaries).
Writing materials for each team.

Duration   2 hours maximum.

Procedure
1. Ask each team to design a game or exercise for the other team(s). The game or exercise must last no longer than 10 minutes. It must be described in writing.
2. The teams have 1 hour to design and write up their games or exercises. You could suggest the exercise format in this book as a documentation template.
3. The games or exercises are then played and reviewed.

Review   There are two aspects to the review. The first is a review of the games or exercises, their effectiveness, and their success at achieving their purpose. Were the procedures or rules clear?
The second is a review of how the team members worked together in developing the game or exercises.

Variations   None, but you may have acquired a new game or two for your collection.

21   Leader of the Band

Description   Teams construct musical instruments from whatever materials they can find, and play a well known tune.

Purpose   This is a creative and team working exercise.

Materials   None. The team members must find what they need.

Duration   About 3 minutes for each performance. An hour or two is needed to construct the instruments and rehearse. This is best done as an overnight exercise.

Procedure   1.   At a plenary session, tell the teams that they are bands whose instruments have been lost at the airport. Rather than disappoint their fans, the bands will make their own instruments from whatever materials they can find, and perform one popular tune.
2.   After the instruments have been constructed, each group performs its tune.

Review   Not necessary.

Variations   1.   Hold the performances on the last evening of a week-long course.
2.   Draw from a container pieces of paper on which are written the names of well-known tunes such as *Three Blind Mice, Yellow Submarine.*

22 Plane Makers

Description Teams design and manufacture paper aeroplanes the performance of which will determine each teams' profit or loss.

Purpose The exercise develops team working and communication, and the making of simple business decisions about the purchase of raw materials and the maximization of profits. There are also opportunities for experimentation, creativity, innovation and learning throughout the exercise.

Materials A ream (500 sheets) of A4 (or letter size) sheets of paper (different colours for each team to aid identification are useful).
Pencils.
Rules.
Paper clips.
Adhesive tape.
Money (this should consist of home made pieces of money, or real 10p pieces or equivalents (see variations); alternatively, keep a record of

income and expenditure for each team during the exercise).
A measuring tape.
Adequate room at least 10 metres (or 33 feet) long.

Duration 40–60 minutes.

Procedure
1. Give each team ten sheets of A4 paper for development purposes.
2. The objective is to design a paper aeroplane that will fly a long distance. The longer the distance is, the more money will be made. After the design phase, there will be a 3 minute production phase during which the team will try to make as many paper aeroplanes to its design as possible. The aeroplanes will then be tested. Therefore, it will be necessary to decide on the production methods during the design phase.
3. Allow the teams a 20 minute design phase.
4. Whilst they are designing the aeroplanes, mark up the test course with 10 feet, 15 feet and 20 feet markers.
5. At the end of the design phase, bring all the teams together and allow them a maximum of three test flights over the course.
6. At the end of testing, the teams have 2 minutes to decide how many planes they will make during the 3 minute production run.
7. The teams purchase the required number of A4 sheets at 1 million Mo per sheet. They may not use sheets from the earlier phase.
8. The teams have a 3 minute production run.
9. The teams bring their completed planes to the course for testing.
10. For every plane that comes to rest beyond the 10 feet (3 metre) marker, the team receives 1 million Mo. For each one beyond the 15 feet (5 metre) marker it receives 2 million Mo, and for each one beyond the 20 feet (7 metre) marker it receives 5 million Mo.
11. The winning team is the one that makes the most money.

Review In addition to the usual team and communication review, also check what strategy each team employed. Did it produce many planes that would fly a short distance, or fewer planes that would fly over 20 feet or more.

Variation Use real money (where 1 million Mo is equivalent to 10p).

23   Role Model

Description   You nominate a particular occupational role, for example 'management consultant', 'customer services manager' or 'airline pilot'. The participants select their 'heroes' or combination of heroes who would be suitable for the role. They then explain to the other members of their group what skills, knowledge and experience their hero(es) or role model(s) would bring to the job.

Purpose   This a creative way of identifying the key attributes of a job.

Materials   A pen for each participant.
Paper for each participant.

Duration   45 or more minutes. This time is very dependent on the size of the group.

Procedure
1.   Give the group the job title and other details of the role you wish to explore. The participants need not have had exposure to the role, but they need to understand its key features. The job title may be sufficient to conjure up an appropriate image.
2.   Once in their small group each participant selects his or her 'heroes', living or dead, who, either individually or in combination, would be expert at the role. The attributes that he or she would bring to the role are listed. This stage takes 20 minutes.
3.   The participants share their findings within their group, and draw up a master list of attributes and 'heroes'.

Review   Lead a discussion on the skills, knowledge and experience needed to undertake various roles. Determine how the groups decided on the key attributes.

Variation   Have the teams present their findings to the whole group, and draw up a composite list of attributes.

24   Safety Audit

Description   Teams perform a safety audit on the location at which the course is being run.

Purpose   This a teamwork exercise that includes reports and presentations.

Materials   None.

Duration   Evening activity.

Procedure
1. Tell the hotel or location management about what you are doing. The team(s) then go round the building(s), and conduct a safety audit of the location.
2. The next day, they present a 5 minute report on their findings.

Review   Discuss how each team tackled the task.

Variations
1. As an amusing and more interesting alternative or addition to the audit, the teams try to find the safest place in the location, and give their reasons for their choice.
2. One team does this exercise whilst another is attempting the challenges (**Sinbad's Challenges**) and a third is doing the review (**TV Anchor**).

25 Sinbad's Challenges

Description   Each team is given a list of challenges to undertake before the sun rises.

Purpose   This is an exercise in creative teamwork.

Materials   A preprepared list of challenges.

Duration   This is normally an evening exercise, but it can be done in course time.

Procedure
1. Preprepare a list of unusual challenges for which creativity, innovation and downright nerve are required, for example collecting unusual objects, or making cliffs whiter.
2. Each team has to carry out its challenges before the sun rises.

Review   Conduct a brief review of how the challenges were completed. Determine how creativity and innovation were used in achieving the targets.

Variation   There are many possible variations, for example selecting the challenges so that they all have a common theme.

26   Strong Bridge

Description Each team builds a bridge that is able to support a series of weights.

Purpose This exercise facilitates team working, communication, and strategy development.

Materials A series of weights (these can be, for example, house bricks or bags of sugar).
Give each team the following materials (the teams must have identical sets of materials, and they need two sets of the materials, one for the design phase and one for the construction phase):
Paper or newspaper (e.g. 10 sheets of flip chart paper or 2 copies of *The Times*).
Card.
Paper clips.
A stapler and staples.
Adhesive tape.

Duration 45 minutes.

Procedure 1. Explain that each team has 30 minutes to design a bridge, followed by 10 minutes to construct it. The bridge must be able to span 20 inches (or 0.5 metres).
2. Explain that the winning team will be the one that has the highest score. The score will be calculated as the load that the bridge can carry without collapsing, divided by the time taken to build the bridge. The load will be measured in ounces (or grams), and the time will be measured in seconds. Thus a bridge built in 5 minutes that can carry more than half of the load of one completed in 10 minutes will have a higher score than the 10 minute bridge.
3. Give each team an identical set of materials, and start the design phase.
4. At the end of the design phase, issue each team with fresh supplies. Start the construction stage, and time each team's construction phase.
5. At the end of the construction phase, load each bridge until it collapses. The weights should be placed on top of each other. Intervals of 0.5 pounds (or 200 grams) are appropriate. (*Note:* If you use as a weight an object, for example a brick, that has an unknown mass, invent a measure. For example, you could say that the mass of one brick is 200 smarg, so that you have sufficiently large numbers to play with.) Always have enough weights, and let a team member load the bridge.

Review   Discuss team roles and how the strategy was decided.

Variation   If a swimming pool or pond is available, ask each team to build a boat rather than a bridge. The boat can have any dimensions. Allow 15 minutes for the construction.

27 Tall Storey

Description   The aim of each team is to build the tallest tower within the time limit.

Purpose   The exercise is a catalyst for team dynamics.

Materials   Give each team the following (the teams must have identical sets of materials):
Sheets of flip chart paper, A3 (or poster size) paper, and A4 (or letter size) paper.
Thin card.
Newspaper.
Paper clips.
A stapler and staples.
Adhesive tape.
A pencil for each participant.
A pair of scissors.

Any other available materials that might be useful in building a tower.

Duration   40 minutes.

Procedure
1. Distribute the sets of materials to the teams. Tell the teams that they have to try to build the tallest tower in the given time.
2. Each team has 30 minutes to plan and build prototypes etc.
3. Each team then has 10 minutes to construct its free standing tower.
4. The winning team is the one that builds the tallest tower in the timescale.

Review   Lead a discussion that examines team dynamics.
Discover what the teams had as their objectives, what the allocated and actual team roles were, and how the task was performed.

Variations
1. All the teams see the other teams' prototype towers before the main build. This can lead to an interesting discussion about undertaking realtime modifications during a manufacturing phase.
2. Specify a minimum height and a load bearing requirement for the towers. Award a bonus for every 1 inch (or 3 centimetres) achieved above the minimum height. As an example, award 1000 points for a 24 inch (or 60 centimetre) tower, and give a bonus of 50 points for every inch over 24 inches. Give no points if the tower fails to support the weight. The weights can be house bricks or something similar, as long as the same weights are used for all the towers. I have used bricks, sugar, tins and a box full of cards.

28   Time Capsule

Description   Participants find items for inclusion in their team's time capsule.

Purpose   This is a creative teamwork exercise.

Materials   One small box per team for the time capsule (something like a shoebox is ideal).

Duration   1 hour (but preferably overnight), followed by 15–20 minutes for presentations.

Procedure   1.   Give each team its time capsule box. Each team must put no more than seven items in the box that would describe the team and its historical period to someone opening the box in 200 years time.
2.   Each team presents the time capsule to the group in a plenary session, explaining why the particular items have been chosen.

Review   A review is only necessary if some themes have emerged that need to be explored.

Variation   Extend the exercise by asking the group to decide which nine items, from all the items selected by the teams, should be placed in a group time capsule.

29   Tower Power

Description   Teams are required to replicate an already constructed tower as quickly as possible.

Purpose   This is a teamwork exercise in which the participants have defined roles and need to cooperate and communicate.

Materials   You need enough coloured building blocks in a variety of shapes and sizes to build $n + 1$ identical towers, where n is the number of teams. Blocks from LEGO® sets or similar construction toys are excellent for this purpose. *Note:* Base plates can help with stability. The tower should be constructed from at least 20 building blocks. Separate rooms are required for each team and for the course leader's tower. Alternatively, each tower can be concealed behind a screen.

Duration   40–60 minutes.

Procedure   1.   In advance of the session, build an irregular tower from blocks of mixed colours and shapes that the teams can replicate after just looking at it. Keep the tower out of sight in a separate room or behind a screen under a cover.
2.   Ask the teams to go to their building areas and decide on the roles that the team members will assume for the exercise. These are as follows. *Builder:* His or her purpose is to construct the tower. This is the only member of the team who is allowed to touch the tower that the team is constructing. *Designer:* His or her purpose is to tell the builder what the tower should look like. This is the only member of the team who is allowed to see your tower. The designer is not allowed to touch either tower. He or she may not take anything into the viewing room with which to record (or transmit) information about the tower. structure. *Negotiator:* His or her purpose is to acquire building pieces with which to construct the tower. The negotiator is the only person who is allowed to communicate with other teams. *Materials controller:* His or her purpose is to determine what materials are required to successfully complete the tower.
3.   Mix all the pieces for making all of the teams' towers together, and separate them into n sets, each of which contain the same number of pieces. (You may wish to ensure that each team has the same number of correct pieces in their set.)
4.   Ask the negotiators from each team to come and collect their building materials. Ask the designers to come and see your tower.
5.   Typically, the following process then occurs within each team. The designer tells the builder and the materials controller what the

tower looks like. The materials controller determines the building block surpluses and shortages, and tells the negotiator. The negotiator acquires new pieces by swapping blocks with other teams. This cycle is usually repeated several times.

6. When a team believes that it has built the tower correctly, the designer takes it to the room where your tower is located for checking. If it is incorrect, the tower is demolished and a 200 second penalty is incurred.

Review   Team roles, communication, and interteam competition versus co-operation are all fertile areas for discussion.

Variations   1.   Have a selection of building blocks for sale at 100Mo per block with each team having 500Mo to spend. A Mo is equivalent to 1.5 seconds. The amount (of time) spent is added to the actual construction time.

2.   Use real money, with a block costing £1 and a £2 fine being incurred for an incorrectly built tower. The winning team takes the pot. This can give the exercise a real edge, but do not expect intergroup cooperation. During a similar exercise, I once saw all the other teams gang up on the one that looked like winning the game. In that instance, no team won.

30 TV Anchor

Description Each team takes it in turn to produce a creative review of the previous day's work.

Purpose This exercise anchors the previous day's work and practises team building.

Materials Whatever the team members can find.

Duration This exercise is done over night, and each team spends as much time as it needs. The actual review should last 3–5 minutes.

Procedure
1. Select the order of the teams by drawing lots, or let the teams decide which order they will go in.
2. Explain that each team is a team of newscasters and reporters that has to fill a 3–5 minute news slot with a review of the previous day's course. *Note:* Humour always helps in this exercise.
3. The teams prepare their reviews overnight, and present them the next day.

Review None.

Variation   Weather forecasting and sports commentating, or a combination of these have worked well.

31   Underneath the Arches

Description   Teams compete to construct four arches in the fastest possible time at the least possible cost.

Purpose   The exercise is primarily concerned with teamwork and negotiation skills.

Materials   You need 28 building blocks for each team. Each team's pieces should be a different colour. LEGO®, or better still DUPLO®, are excellent, and the larger the pieces are, the better. Each arch is constructed of six cubes (three for each pillar), and a bridging piece, and so each team's four arches require $4 \times 7 = 28$ blocks. You also need a stop watch, a bag or box to hold the pieces to be auctioned, and 150 home made 10Mo notes.

Duration   30 minutes.

Procedure

1. Mix up all the pieces, and give a representative from each team a set of 16 building blocks, comprising eight pieces of his or her own team's colour and eight other coloured pieces, and 300Mo (30 10Mo notes) of currency. You retain the rest of the pieces for auctioning.
2. The participants have 25 minutes to build their four arches. They may trade amongst themselves or buy pieces at auction.
3. Auctions are held 5 minutes, 10 minutes, 15 minutes and 20 minutes after the start of the exercise. The timing of the auctions must be precise. Start the auction whether anybody is there or not. Explain the bidding rules. If no-one attends the auction, it opens and closes immediately. Pieces are drawn at random from a box or bag (you must not be able to see them). The bidding always starts at 20Mo. If no-one bids, the piece is offered at 10Mo. The auction stops as soon as there are no bids for the piece displayed. To bid, a bidder must raise his or her hand and state the value of the bid. The person who bids the most for a piece is deemed to be the purchaser. The auctioneer makes a note of the successful bidders, and at the end of the auction the successful bidders settle up. Any bidder who has insufficient money to complete the deal is not allowed any pieces, and his or her team is barred from the next auction. The auctioneer's decision is final.
4. The winning team is the one that has the highest score. The score is the money that the team has left divided by the time taken to build the team's arches. The money is in Mos, and the time is measured in minutes.

Review   Review strategies as well as team roles and effectiveness. Discuss negotiations and buying at auction.

Variations   None.

III

Large group exercises

The exercises in this chapter are for six or more participants, and most work well for up to 24. There are times during a lecture session when you notice participants' eyes beginning to glaze over. As trainers know only too well, if you have more than a minute or two's input left to give at this point, you are wasting your breath, and 'time out' should be called. Rather than just having a leg stretch or coffee or cigarette break, run a short exercise to start the blood moving again. The exercises in this section can be used as pure energizers. Most of them also introduce large group puzzle or problem solving and creativity. However, probably most importantly, they should be fun, and they are usually accompanied by much talking and laughter.

Look around and see what resources are close to hand for your energizer. A colleague of mine, Jo Anne Freeman, described to me how the idea for **My Precious** came from needing to run an energizer when the only resource she had available was a bowl of fruit.

32   Bizarre Bazaar

Description Participants select an object which they have to sell to another member of the group.

Purpose This exercise is an energizer which also releases creative potential.

Materials You need a box of everyday objects, for example bath plugs, candles and springs. There should be more objects than participants so that they have a choice.

Duration 10 minutes.

Procedure
1. Pass the box around the group, and ask everybody to take one object.
2. Participants then have 2 minutes to examine their object thoroughly, noting its texture, colour, shape and so on. They must think of different and original uses that the object might have.
3. Ask the participants to rise to their feet, and tell them that they have brought their precious objects to the bazaar to sell. Ask them to walk around the bazaar greeting others as they pass by.
4. After 1 minute of this, call out 'stop', and ask the participants to pair up with the person nearest to him or her.
5. The pairs decide which of them will speak first. Each person then has 1 minute to influence the other to buy his or her precious object. After 1 minute, tell the pairs to switch roles. (If there is an odd number of participants, have one group of three, each of whom has 40 seconds to make his or her pitch).

Review Talk about the need for doing limbering up exercises prior to undertaking a problem solving exercise.

Variations None.

33   Coining It In

Description   Each participant attempts to position his or her coin closest to a spot on the table or floor.

Purpose   This is a large group energizer and creativity exercise.

Materials   A 2p coin or equivalent for each person (tell the participants before the game to bring one, and have some change for those who forget).
Chalk, or a dry wipe marker.
Construction materials such as flip chart paper, newspaper, adhesive tape, paper clips, and a stapler and staples.
A measuring tape.

Duration   20 minutes.

Procedure   *Phase 1:*
1. Draw a circle around a 2p coin, either on the floor, or on a large table (around 5 feet in length).
2. Draw a line on the floor that is 4.5 feet (or 1.4 metres) in front of the coin, or place the coin at this distance from one end of the table. If the floor is carpeted or cannot be marked, use tape or string to create the line, and use a 50p coin as the target.
3. Ask each participant to stand behind the line or at the end of the table and slide, toss or roll his or her coin as close to the target as possible.
4. Make a note of the winner(s), and the general level of accuracy of the group.

Phase 2:
5. Using whatever materials are to hand, each participant has 10 minutes to construct a 'tool' that will improve his or her accuracy.
6. Make a note of the winners, and general level of accuracy of the group.

Review   Lead a discussion on how participants solved the problem.

Variation   For the second phase, organize the group into teams of three or four to solve the problem. Allow 20 minutes for constructing the tool.

34   Cooperative Circle

Description   The group of participants form a circle. They hold hands and support each other as alternate members lean inwards and outwards.

Purpose   This is a large group cooperative energizer.

Materials   None.

Duration   5 minutes.

Procedure
1. 10–12 people is ideal for this exercise. It can become more difficult as the number becomes larger, but try it anyway and see. Ask the participants to stand in a circle. Number them off in twos around the circle. Ask the participants to hold hands.
2. Ask the odd numbers to keep their bodies as straight as possible and lean towards the centre of the circle, and the even ones to lean away from the centre. Each person should counterbalance his or her neighbours.
3. Repeat the process with the even numbers leaning in and the odd numbers leaning out.

Review   Review cooperation and trust.

Variations   None.

35   Cumulative Pull Up

Description   The group of participants sit down, link hands, and attempt to stand up as one unit.

Purpose   This is a cooperative and creative exercise.

Materials   None.

Duration   5–10 minutes, depending on the number in the group.

Procedure
1. Ask the participants to pair off. (Have one group of three if there is an odd number of participants.)
2. Ask the pairs to sit facing each other (a group of three forms a triangle). The pairs link hands, and, by pulling on each other, stand up together.
3. When the exercise has been completed with pairs, ask the pairs to make fours, and repeat the exercise. If there is an odd pair, add it to a four to attempt a six stand up.
4. Combine the fours to make eights and repeat.
5. If they are not already doing so, suggest that the groups experiment with grips, for example gripping wrists and forearms, to help them stand up.
6. Continue the exercise until the group discovers the largest number of participants who can combine to complete a cooperative pull up.

Review   Discuss trust, cooperation, leadership and creative holds.

Variations   None.

Learning Resources
Centre

36   Human Knot

Description   The group of participants link hands to form a human knot. They then unravel themselves.

Purpose   This is an exercise in large group interaction and puzzle solving.

Materials   None.

Duration   10 minutes.

Procedure
1. Ask the participants to form a tight huddle.
2. Ask them to raise their right hands. Then ask them to reach across the huddle and grasp the right hand of another person.
3. Ask them to raise their left hands. Then ask them to reach across the huddle and grasp the left hand of another person. This should not be the same person as the first person they joined hands with.
4. *You* then break one link. The participants then have to unravel themselves into one line without breaking the other links.

Review   Review the management of the unravelling process.

Variations   None. However, this also makes a hilarious party game when people have had a few alcoholic drinks.

37   Just a Minute

Description   Each participant is required to estimate a 2 minute time span.

Purpose   This a good exercise for quietening a group down, and for examining group norms.

Materials   A watch.
A preprepared sheet with a list of times from 30 to 150 seconds, and space for names against the times (or, better still, a video camera focused on the whole group, with the date and time superimposed on the tape).
Something to obscure the faces of all the clocks in the room.

Duration   3 minutes.

Procedure

1. Ask the participants to estimate a time span of 2 minutes without looking at their watches.
2. They indicate that they think that the 2 minutes are up by raising their hands and keeping them up. They need not raise their hands very high above their heads.
3. You record the time elapsed for each participant (ask someone to help you spot the raised hands).

Review   An interesting discussion can be held about the pressure felt by each participant as hands started to be raised ahead of his or her estimate.

Variations   None.

38   Knee Sit

Description   The group of participants form a circle. Each participant sits on the knee of the person behind him or her in the circle until everyone is sitting on someone's knee.

Purpose   This is an exercise in solving a large group puzzle, and introducing cooperation and care for others.

Materials   None.

Duration   5 minutes.

Procedure   1.   Form the group of participants into a circle.
              2.   Ask all the participants to face clockwise and grasp the waist of the person in front of them. They then all take one side step towards the centre of the circle.

3. Tell the participants to place themselves in a sitting position so that each person is sitting on the knee of the person behind, with the person in front sitting on his or her knee.

Review   Discuss the process used to solve the problem and the need for trust.

Variations None.

39   Mini Aerobics

Description   All the participants do some simple exercises.

Purpose   This is a pure energizer.

Materials   None.

Duration   5 minutes.

Procedure   1.   Ask all the participants to rise to their feet.
2.   Lead some easy exercises, for example stretching, touching toes, and circling arms.

Review   None.

Variation   This can become a regular session with different participants leading the aerobics.

40 My Precious (With apologies to Tolkien)

Description Each participant is given an object with which he or she has to familiarize himself or herself. He or she then has to find the object in a group of similar objects.

Purpose This is an energizer that focuses on observational skills and people's ability to make distinctions.

Materials As many very similar objects as there are participants (fruit or vegetables are excellent, for example carrots or oranges).

Duration 5 minutes.

Procedure
1. Give each participant an object. Explain that each object is precious to the participant examining it.
2. Allow participants 2 minutes to examine their objects thoroughly. Participants must not mark the objects.
3. Collect up the objects and place them on a table in the middle of the group.
4. Ask the participants to find their own precious objects.

Review Discuss how the participants determined what the distinctive features of their object were. You can mention that it is said that Eskimos can recognize 23 different types of snow – their lives depend upon it. A discussion can be led into how we make distinctions in our lives.

Variation Remove one or more objects from the group of objects after you have collected them. There can be interesting individual dynamics. Ask any person without an object what its distinguishing features were.

41   Paper Frisbee

Description   The participants play Frisbee games using paper plates.

Purpose   This is a large group energizer.

Materials   A paper plate for each participant plus an additional one (the best plates are the deeper dessert ones).

Duration   10 minutes.

Procedure
1. Give each participant a paper plate. He or she should write his or her name on the plate.
2. Place the extra paper plate about 15 feet (or 4.6 metres) away. The participants have to position their own plates as close as possible to

the target. It is best for the participants to take turns rather than for them all to throw their plates at once, but a free for all can be fun!

Review   None.

Variations   1. Plate golf is an outside (or large hall) exercise. Push ten (nine plus a start post) garden canes into the ground to make a 'golf course' (the canes should be 4 feet (or 1.2 metres) long). You can put flags on them if you wish. As with normal golf the participants play in pairs. To commence the game each person stands beside the start post and skims his or her plate towards the first 'hole'. He or she counts how many throws are taken to hit the cane. Each player takes it in turns to throw with each verifying the other's score. When he or she has hit the first cane, he or she stands beside it and skims the plate towards the second cane. This continues until the course has been completed. The winner is the person who completes the course in the least number of throws.

   2. You can also have a plate decorating competition before the event.

42   Spoof

Description   The participants play a simple guessing game which can have a high personal cost.

Purpose   This is a mild energizer.

Materials   Five coins or five matches for each participant.

Duration   This very dependent on the size of the group.

Procedure
1. The participants sit in a circle facing the centre. They decide who is going to start.
2. The action moves in a clockwise direction. The person starting, the 'guesser', turns to face the person on his or her left. This person puts his or her hands behind his or her back, and puts a number (from one to five) of coins or matches in his or her right hand. This hand is then clenched and held out towards the guesser.
3. The guesser states how many coins or matches he or she thinks are in the neighbour's hand. If the guess is incorrect then the guesser is out of the game.
4. Play moves on clockwise, with the neighbour becoming the guesser. It continues until only person remains.

Review   Discuss how participants felt when they guessed right or wrong, and the pressures that they felt as the number remaining in the game decreased.

Variations   None.

43   Stereotypes

Description   The participants are shown pictures of people cut from magazines and asked to describe them.

Purpose   The exercise explores stereotypes and prejudices.

Materials   Cut 8–10 photographs of people out of magazines. The people should not be famous. Try to include a well dressed villain, for example a convicted bank robber or murderer, and people from minorities and both genders. A picture of a scruffily dressed multimillionaire is also a good one to include. However, you do not need to know any of the people's backgrounds for the exercise to work; if you do, it just makes it even more powerful. You also need a pen and paper for each participant.

Duration   30–40 minutes.

Procedure
1. Number and display the pictures, or, if you are working with a small group, give one photograph to each participant.
2. The participants spend 10 minutes looking at the photographs, and make any notes they wish. In a small group, all the photographs can be passed round at the end of each minute.
3. The leader points to each picture in turn, or holds them up one at a time, and asks what the participants can say about the person in the picture. Typically, the descriptions start with a few facts, which are then followed by a great many value judgements. The leader captures the main observations. The leader may need to give some prompts, such as 'what do you think he or she does for a living?' or 'what sort of car or house might he or she own?'.
4. After all the photographs have been shown, the leader revisits each one, and asks the participants how they arrived at the observations. The group discuss what truths can be determined from the picture, and what cannot. The group can then talk about preconceptions and prejudices, particularly those experienced when seeing or meeting someone for the first time.

Review   This is part of the exercise.

Variations   None.

44   Sudden Death

Description   The participants form a line along a 'precipice'. They then have to arrange themselves in a specific order without any team member 'dying'.

Purpose   This is an exercise in large group cooperative puzzle solving. It also puts the participants into the personal space of the others.

Materials   You need a builder's plank (or two strips of masking tape stuck on the floor 11 inches (or 28 centimetres) apart). The plank (or the lines) should be long enough for all the participants to be able to stand on the plank (or between the lines). You also need a stop watch (optional).

Duration   10 minutes for a group of around 15 people. If there are 16 or more people, split them into two teams and have a race (the winning team is then the one that completes the task in the shortest time without loss of life).

Procedure   1.   Ask the participants to stand on the plank (or between the lines). Then explain that they are standing on a precipice with a drop of 1000 feet (or 300 metres) on either side. To step off the plank or lines is certain death. The participants must arrange themselves in order of the darkness of their eyes, that is, from very pale blue to very dark brown. A successful outcome to the exercise is when they arrange themselves in the correct order without loss of life.
2.   Give the participants 10 minutes to complete the exercise if there are around 15 of them, or less time if the group is smaller. Then, if time permits, ask them to rearrange themselves in the reverse order.
3.   *Note:* Do not use eye colour in countries in which almost all the eye colours are similar, for example Africa.

Review   Discuss large group puzzle solving in terms of how was it managed and how the process was determined. Talk about how communication down the line was achieved. Discuss group learning if the exercise was done a second time or there were two teams.

Variations   1.   Ask the participants to arrange themselves in height order.
2.   Ask the participants to arrange themselves in height order while blindfolded

45   Table Manners

Description   The participants must fit as many people as possible onto a table.

Purpose   This is a cooperative exercise.

Materials   A large, strong table.

Duration   5 minutes.

Procedure
1. Tell the participants that they have 5 minutes to fit as many people onto the table as possible.
2. The group of people on the table must not touch the ground for at least 15 seconds.
3. Stress to the participants that are responsible for each other's safety.

Review   Consider how the exercise was conducted. Who gave instructions, and how did the participants help each other?

Variations
1. Have a competition between two teams, using two smaller tables.
2. Use a number of smaller tables, and conduct the exercise like musical chairs, with a table being removed each time. Competition should give way to cooperation.

46   Wallyball

Description   This a seated version of volleyball that uses balloons.

Purpose   The exercise is a large group energizer.

Materials   Two large round balloons.
String.
Two tables.
Two chairs.
A chair for each participant.

Duration   3 minutes per game.

Procedure
1. Split the group into two teams. Sit each team in two rows of chairs so that one team's two rows face the other team's two rows. The front rows of the two teams should be 5 feet (or 1.5 metres) apart, and there should be 3 feet (or 1 metre) between each team's front and back row.
2. Use the two tables, two chairs and string to make a 'net' about 4 feet (or 1.2 metres) from the ground between the two teams.
3. The object of the game is for the balloons to land on the opposing team's ground. The team members must remain seated at all times during the game. They can only hit a balloon with their hands. A balloon must go over the net to score a point.
4. To start a game, gently tap a balloon towards each team. Keep the score.
5. The winning team is the one that scores the most goals in 3 minutes.

Review   None.

Variation   Tap in another eight balloons after 1 minute. The game should become fast and furious.

47   Who Am I?

Description   A competition takes place between two or more teams. The names of two members of a team are drawn from a container by another team. The drawing team then has to mime a person whose name has been drawn so that the other team(s) can guess who he or she is.

Purpose   This is an exercise in observation and feedback from individuals. It also develops creativity.

Materials   A pen for each participant.
Paper for each participant.
A small box or similar container.

Duration   This varies with the size of the group. Allow at least 45 minutes.

Procedure   1.   Form small teams of four or more people.
2.   Each team member writes his or her name on a piece of paper, folds the paper, and places it in the central container.
3.   Once everybody's name has been put in the container it is passed to a representative of each team, who selects a paper from the container. If they select the name of a person in their team the paper is replaced and the representative draws again.
3.   The teams separate, and spend 5 minutes listing three facts about the person whose names they have drawn, and thinking about their mimes.
4.   The teams reconvene, and the order of the mimes is agreed. The first mime is performed. The members of the other teams discuss who they believe it is, and then make one guess per team. If the guess is wrong, the miming team gives one clue, and does the mime again. The other teams discuss the mime again and make a second guess. This process continues until one of the other teams guesses the name correctly. If the name cannot be guessed correctly the name is given and the group move on to the next team to commence their mime.
5.   If time permits each team my draw another name from the box and repeat the exercise.

Review   Lead a discussion on observation and characters.

Variation   Instead of a mime, the team just give facts about the person, one at a time, and the other teams then guess who the subject is.

IV

Individual exercises

Individual exercises are not particularly energizing. They primarily focus on skills development or the introduction of a concept. I have often used the **Nine Dots** or **Match Triangles** exercises before a large group discussion on problem solving and the need to look beyond the predefined boundaries. In addition to just being fun, **Yes, But ...** and **Business Kim** can introduce creativity and mind mapping, respectively. **Mind Power** is pure fun, and participants are often genuinely surprised when the paper clip begins to rotate.

    60 Second Opportunity often starts an individual's adrenaline flowing, and it can be used to ensure a prompt return from breaks.

48   Beans In a Jar

Description   This is an example of the use of a Delphi method for prediction (see Author's Note at the end of the exercise). A large number of beans are placed in a jar and each participant estimates how many beans there are in the jar. The guesses are displayed for all the participants to see. The process is repeated a further three times. The average of the last set of estimates is then calculated and compared with the actual number of beans.

Purpose   This exercise is a simple introduction and illustrative approach to the Delphi method of prediction. The variations enable participants to observe how the level of accuracy changes with the modified approaches. Use different sizes of beans and/or jars (or pieces of string, rope or pole) for the variations.

Materials   A jar filled with beans (previously counted).
A pen for each participant.
Paper for each participant.

Duration   15 minutes.

Procedure
1. Place the bean jar in full view of the participants. Allow the participants to examine the jar.
2. Ask each participant to write down in silence his or her estimate of the number of beans in the jar.
3. Collect up the estimates. Display the estimates for all the participants to see.
4. Repeat this process three times.
5. Calculate the mean of the last set of estimates, where the mean is the sum of the estimates divided by the number of estimates. Compare the calculated mean with the actual number of beans in the jar.

Review   Discuss the estimating processes used, examine their accuracy, and describe the Delphi approach to forecasting.

Variations
1. After the second estimate, ask if anyone wishes to say why they think the highest estimate is incorrect, and then ask if anyone wishes to say why they think the lowest estimate is incorrect. There should be no other discussion amongst the participants.
2. Having done the first variation, allow general discussion after the third round of estimates, that is, before the final round of estimates.
3. Estimate the length of a piece of rope instead of guessing the number of beans in a jar.

Author's Note: The Delphi technique, a method of developing group consensus was originally used at the RAND Corporation to arrive at reliable predictions about the future of technology. The traditional Delphi approach poses questions/interrogations about an issue which are sent to experts in that particular field. The experts do not meet but respond to the session moderator. The moderator summarises all the responses and feeds back the anonymous summaries to the participants. The individual participant then has the opportunity to revise his or her own opinions and ratings. It has been found that no matter how antagonistic the initial positions or complex the questions under analysis that competing opinions often converge and synthesise using this technique.

Whilst the Delphi is most frequently used with experts at arms length I have successfully used it as a facilitation tool in a workshop environment to quickly obtain 'ball park' consensus, particularly if I am interested in numeric data. For example I might pose the question, 'What is the likely market share for Widgets in 2001?' **Beans In a Jar** is a good warm up exercise before the 'difficult' questions are posed.

49 Business Kim

Description	The participants have to memorize everyday business items.
Purpose	This is a memory exercise.
Materials	20 everyday business items (which should be covered or kept in a separate room). A pencil for each participant. Paper for each participant.
Duration	10 minutes.
Procedure	1. Show the 20 objects to the participants for 2 minutes. Cover them. 2. Give the participants 3 minutes to remember them and write them down.
Review	Lead a discussion on the memory strategies employed and mind mapping (see Author's Note at the end of the exercise).
Variations	1. Remove three objects from the group of objects. Ask the participants what has been removed. 2. Replace five objects in the group of objects with different ones. Ask the participants what has been changed. 3. Rearrange five objects in the group of objects. Ask the participants what has been changed.

Author's Note: Mind Mapping was developed by Tony Buzan as a way of logically capturing and structuring ideas. He has written a number of books on this subject which include a training video, 'Mind Power with Tony Buzan' published by the BBC.

50   I Like Coffee

Description   The participants try to determine the rule of the game.

Purpose   I have used this exercise to amuse the group when conversation appears to have dried up. It can also be used to illustrate how someone feels when he or she is not part of a group that he or she wishes to belong to.

Materials   None.

Duration   This is extremely variable, and it depends on the size of the group and the speed with which the participants grasp the rule. Generally, the exercise should not go on for more than about 15–20 minutes. If one or two people still have not worked out the rule at that point, it is worth closing off and discussing how they felt. Be sensitive.

Procedure
1. Make the statement 'I like coffee but I don't like tea'. Follow this with other statements in which there is a double letter in one of the nouns but not the other. The nouns in each statement should be related, for example they could be beverages, planets, or people's names (as in 'I like Jenny but I don't like Jean').
2. If nobody guesses what the game is, stop and explain that you want them to discover what rule you are using to construct your statements. When they have, they must join in and make statements of their own that obey the rule.
3. If an incorrect statement is made, state which nouns you like or do not like, for example by saying 'no, I don't like peas or beans'.
4. The exercise continues until everybody understands the rule or until you explain the rule.
5. *Note:* People can become very frustrated if they are unable to find the rule. This may need to be managed, particularly if unhelpful comments are being made by other members of the group.

Review   Lead a discussion on how participants identified the rule. Find out how long after having spotted it they felt confident enough to test it out for themselves.
Discuss with the last few people to spot the rule how they felt when everyone else had worked out the rule and they had not. If you observed interesting behaviours by those who knew the rule and those who did not, follow this up with the group.

Variations   None.

51   Mind Power

Description   The participants use their 'mind power' to make a paper clip rotate.

Purpose   This is a fun exercise.

Materials   A piece of string or thread that is 2 feet (or 0.6 metres) long for each participant.
A paper clip for each participant.

Duration   5 minutes.

Procedure
1. Give each participant a length of string and a paper clip.
2. Each participant ties his or her paper clip to one end of the piece of string. The participant holds the end of the piece of string between his or her thumb and first or second finger. The paper clip is suspended and held in a stationary position.
3. Instruct the participants to focus on their paper clips and think about it rotating. They must not move the hand that is holding the paper clip.
4. The paper clips rotate.

Review   Ask the participants for an explanation of the phenomenon. *Explanation*: When the participant is focusing on the paper clip, his or her thumb and finger move imperceptibly. This very slight movement is amplified by the length of string, and the paper clip rotates.

Variation   Ask the participants to rotate the paper clip clockwise and then anti-clockwise.

52   Nine Dots

Description The participants are required to join up nine dots with four straight lines.

Purpose This is a lateral thinking exercise that introduces thinking 'outside the box'.

Materials A pen or pencil for each participant.
Paper for each participant.
An overhead projector or a flip chart that shows the nine dots.

Duration 5 minutes.

Procedure 1. Draw nine dots as shown in the diagram.

2. Ask each participant to copy the dots onto a piece of paper. He or she must then join up the nine dots using four straight lines. The pen or pencil must not leave the paper.
3. The most obvious solution is shown in the second diagram.

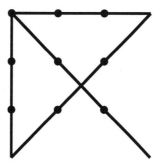

4. *Note:* There are also some other, very creative, solutions. A participant could use a very thick pen that would pass through several dots at once, or fold the paper so that there was only a small gap between the dots. Do not refer to these other solutions in advance,

but pose them as a problem to those who have done the nine dot exercise before, or finished it very quickly.

Review   This is an exercise in thinking 'outside the box'. Lead a discussion on testing the boundaries of the problem. Also, discuss rules which constrain the solution of a problem.

Variations   None

53   60 Second Opportunity

Description   This is a 60 second role play in which the leader plays the role of managing director, and a participant plays a salesperson, consultant, or middle manager who meets him or her by the lift.

Purpose   This is an exercise in thinking creatively on your feet.

Materials   None.

Duration   1 minute.

Procedure   1. Select a participant, or use a rule which selects a participant, for example late arrival at the session.
2. The leader plays the role of the managing director of the participant's company or the MD of a company with which the participant wishes to conduct business. The MD is waiting for the lift, and the participant also arrives at the lift. The objective of the exercise is for the participant to ensure that the MD is so interested in what the participant has to say that he or she will want to meet with the participant again.
3. If the participant fails to initiate a conversation, the MD says 'aren't you X from Y – how are things going?'. The conversation then continues for 60 seconds.

Review   Carry out a brief review of the *positive* areas of the conversation. You can also consider stress levels and feelings.

Variations   None.

54   Match Triangles

Description   Each participant has to make four equilateral triangles from six matches without breaking them.

Purpose   This is an exercise in thinking 'outside the box'.

Materials   Six matches for each participant.

Duration   5 minutes.

Procedure
1. If the participants are not sitting at tables, ask them to place a flat surface, for example a book, on their laps.
2. Give each participant six matches, and ask the participants to lay them out in a row in front of them on their book or table.

3. Ask the participants to make four equilateral triangles from their matches without breaking the matches. *There should be no shapes other than equilateral triangles* in their solution.

4. *Hint for leader:* The solution is a pyramid with a triangular base.

Review Lead a discussion about reframing problems. By asking the participants to lay the matches out in front of them, the leader suggests that the problem is a two dimensional one, and that the solution lies in one plane. Discuss looking beyond the obvious solutions.

Variations None.

55   Yes, But ...

Description   This is a 'brainstorming' style exercise in which participants have to think of all the possible reasons why they should not do something.

Purpose   This is an exercise in using creative avoidance creatively.

Materials   A pencil for each delegate.
Paper for each delegate.

Duration   5 minutes for individuals, and 10 minutes if the participants are in teams.

Procedure   1.   Name a task such as mowing the lawn, visiting relatives, or decorating the kitchen. Tell the participants that they have been asked to undertake this task.
2.   The participants have to think of as many reasons why they should not do the task as possible in 3 minutes. Each person suggests his or her most creative idea. If the participants are working in teams, let the group decide which are the three most creative ideas.

Review   No review is necessary as such. However, you could explain the need for people to warm up their creative 'muscles' before commencing a problem solving exercise.

Variations   None.

V

Paired exercises

When running people development training, I always like to include some paired work as well as individual, team and large group exercises. In paired work, you can focus on communication, and in particular on questioning, listening and responding skills. I was introduced to **Get Knotted** at a New Year's Eve party when the impact of alcohol on our problem solving capabilities was only too apparent. Chris Lever, with whom I trained for many years, developed **Drawing Backwards** when we were looking for a different way to explore questioning and listening.

You can also use a number of the team exercises for pairs. The exercise would then be purely a problem solving one, as two people are unlikely to generate a great deal of group dynamics data.

Sometimes, if some pairings are unable to work together, or even know each other too well, you will find it necessary to engineer the pairings.

56   Drawing Backwards

Description   A pair of participants sit back to back. One of the pair is given a picture, and then describes it to the other. The partner tries to reproduce the picture without having seen it.

Purpose   This exercise explores and develops questioning and listening skills.

Materials   Photocopies of two prepared drawings (preferably, one should be made up from geometric shapes, and the other should have a more biological content) (each set of photocopies should be enough for half the participants).
A pencil for each participant.
Paper for each participant.

Duration   30 minutes.

Procedure   1.   Sit the pairs back to back in a row. Space the pairs out along the length of the room so that there is some space between the pairs.
2.   Hand a drawing to one half of each pair. All the recipients should be on the same side of the row.
3.   The other member of the pair has 10 minutes to ask questions about the drawing and attempt to replicate it.
4.   Stop the exercise and ask the pairs to compare the picture with the drawing.
5.   Repeat the exercise by reversing the roles and using the other drawing.

Review   The review should cover questioning skills, open and closed questions, and checking understanding.

Variations   None.

57   **Get Knotted**

Description   The wrists of pairs of participants are tied together. The participants have to free themselves without untying the string.

Purpose   This is a paired puzzle on cooperative working.

Materials   2 feet (or 0.6 metres) of parcel string for each participant.

Duration   10 minutes

Procedure   1.   The participants work in pairs. One of the pair ties the ends of a piece of string to both of his or her wrists. The other person ties his or her piece of string to one wrist. This person then feeds the loose end of the string between the other's string and body, and then ties it to his or her other wrist. The two participants are then tied together. They should not be tied too tightly, to avoid constricting the participants' circulations. *Note:* It is easier to demonstrate this than explain it in words.

2. The pairs then have to free themselves without untying themselves or cutting the string.

3. *Solution:* Take a loop of one person's string. Feed it through the string tied round one of his or her partner's wrists. Then take it over the partner's hand and back through the string round the partner's wrist.

Review   Lead a discussion about cooperative problem solving. Consider how each pair did or did not discover the solution.

Variations   None.

58   Hand To Hand

Description   The participants work in pairs with their right hands touching. One person moves his or her hand around, and the partner tries to stay in contact.

Purpose   This is an exercise in being responsive to one's partner.

Materials   None.

Duration   10 minutes.

Procedure
1. Pair off the participants.
2. The pairs stand facing each other about 2 feet (or 0.6 metres) apart. Their arms are slightly raised, and the backs of their right hands are lightly touching. The pairs agree who will go first.
3. One of the pair moves his or her hand around slowly. The partner tries to stay in contact. The pairs should also attempt to do this with their eyes closed and with reducing pressure.
4. The partners should change places after about 5 minutes.

Review   Lead a general discussion on how the exercise worked. Consider following and leading behaviours and being responsive.

Variations   None.

59 Negotiate To Close

Description This is a paired negotiation exercise in which one person attempts to convince another that he or she should do something that he or she would rather not do.

Purpose This exercise explores negotiation skills and creative avoidance.

Materials The observers may require pen and paper.

Duration 15 minutes.

Procedure
1. Sort the participants into threes.
2. Ask the groups of three to decide which one of them will be the manager, who will play the employee, and who will observe.
3. Set up the role play conditions. There is one observer in each group. One of the other two is a manager, and the other is a member of his or her staff. The manager wants the member of staff to work until 9.00 p.m. to deal with an urgent order. The member of staff has an appointment at 7.00 p.m. The three people position themselves to negotiate or observe.
4. The manager has 5 minutes to obtain the employee's agreement to working late. The observer notes what occurs.
5. The three participants then discuss what happened.
6. If there is time, the roles can be rotated.

Review Consider what happened in each group of three, and the strategies used to elicit agreement and to avoid having to work late. Explore how different types of people respond in this type of situation. The observations are very important.

Variation Use a different scenario, for example smokers and nonsmoking zones.

60   Trust Me!

Description   This is an exercise in cooperative working. One person guides his or her blindfolded partner around a series of obstacles.

Purpose   The exercise introduces cooperative working, trust, communication and language.

Materials   A blindfold for half of the participants.
Several chairs.

Duration   10 minutes.

Procedure
1. Pair up the participants.
2. One partner is the other's guide. The guides go to one end of the room, and the partners put on blindfolds.
3. Place chairs to act as obstacles (mines) between the guides and the people with the blindfolds.
4. On the word 'go', the guides have to give verbal instructions to their partners so that they can negotiate the obstacles without hitting them. Ten points are awarded for each hit, and after five hits the pair is out.
5. The pair with the lowest score is the winner. If there is a tie for the lowest score, the team that is first home wins.

Review   Discuss feelings, language, interference (noise) and distance.

Variation   Conduct the same exercise, one pair at a time. You can discuss differences and learning. Allow 2 minutes for the person in the blindfold to cross the room.

61 Yes, And ...

Description Pairs of participants hold a conversation. Each person builds on what the other has just said, prefixing his or her comment with 'yes, and ...'.

Purpose This is a communication exercise in listening and building.

Materials None.

Duration 10 minutes.

Procedure
1. Pair up the participants. If possible, pair each person with someone else from his or her organization. The pairs should sit so that they can converse comfortably. (You can even have a discussion on this if you wish.)
2. The conversation must be about 'what I would do if I were managing director of our organization' (or the Prime Minister if the partners are not from the same organization).
3. One of the partners start the conversation. If the other partner wishes to add their comments, they say 'yes', followed by a brief summary of what had been said, followed by 'and ...'.

Review Hold a discussion on communication and building on the other person's ideas. You may also discuss the facial expressions and posture that people display when trying to interrupt and build on their partner's ideas. Consider how natural the interruptions appeared, at first and then later in the conversation.

Variations None

VI

Creative problem solving

During 1994 and 1995, I undertook research into creativity and innovation in UK companies. In the course of the research I discovered a significant gap between what senior executives said about maintaining a creative and innovative culture in their organization and what they actually did. The results indicated that, whilst 20% of respondents said they had a highly creative and innovative organization, only about 2% appeared to actively foster such a culture. However, over 95% of the respondents considered creativity and innovation to be critical for future success.

The exercises in this chapter can help develop skills, and they provide some tools that can give participants a fresh approach to problem solving. They can also be quite energizing. I have often observed participants being initially rather reluctant to try these different ways of exploring a problem. You may need to give them some encouragement or spend a little time explaining hard and soft thinking. They may not have done this sort of thing since they were children and it may feel strange to them at first. However, once they become involved, they are usually extremely enthusiastic.

62   Action Replay

Description   The participants role play a problem.

Purpose   This exercise introduces an alternative way of problem solving creatively.

Materials   None, unless participants require props.

Duration   60 minutes.

Procedure
1. Divide the large group members up into small teams of 4–6 people.
2. Each small team produces a 5 minute play or sketch about a business problem chosen by one of the members of the team. Allow 25 minutes for this stage.
3. Each small team presents their play to the large group. This is followed by a group discussion about the problem and how it might be solved. Allow 15 minutes for this stage of the exercise.

Review   A review should not be necessary except to discuss how the approach worked. The key areas to consider are the discussions that took place whilst the playlet was being developed, and those that occurred after it had been presented.

Variation   Instead of the large group discussion the session can be modified by allowing each team to produce a play depicting their solution to one of the problems presented to the large group. A similar amount of time will be required.

63   Ambiguity Rules?

Description   The participants have to find the hidden word in an ambiguously worded problem statement.

Purpose   This an exercise in how ambiguity can stimulate the imagination.

Materials   A flip chart.
A pencil for each participant.
Paper for each participant.

Duration   5 minutes.

Procedure   1.   Write the following sequence of letters on the flip chart:

OSRIAXLENTGTERES

2.   Ask the participants to write down the sequence and cross out six letters so that the remaining letters, without their sequence being altered, spell a familiar word.
3.   *Answer:* My answer is 'ORANGE'. There may be others.

Review   The problem statement is ambiguous and there may be some other creative answers. Explore how the participants approached the problem and examine how ambiguity can stimulate creative thoughts. My solution removed SIX LETTERS.

Variation   You can hide your own special word, perhaps as a clue to another problem.

64 Card Storm

Description This a variation of brainstorming in which cards or Post-its® are used instead of paper.

Purpose This exercise introduces a technique and helps exercise the participants' creative muscles.

Materials You need coloured cards that measure approximately 8 × 3 inches (or 200 × 75 millimetres) and plastic re-usable adhesive, or large Post-its® that measure 5 × 3 inches (or 127 × 76 millimetres) or 6 × 4 inches (or 152 × 102 millimetres). You also need a marker pen for each participant.

Duration 30 minutes.

Procedure
1. Divide the participants up into small teams.
2. Set a task. For example, ask the participants to think of as many uses as they can for an everyday object, such as a brick or a paper clip.
3. Each team is given 20 minutes to write its ideas down on cards or Post-its®, stick them on a white board or wall, and group them to eliminate duplicates. The team should appoint a member to facilitate or lead this stage. New ideas can then be added at this point.
4. The team counts how many different uses it has identified. It decides which it thinks are the three most creative, and notes the reasons.
5. The teams then reconvene. Each team present its results to the others.

Review Lead a discussion on the use of brainstorming in problem solving.

Variations
1. A follow on exercise can be done in which the teams have 10 minutes to think of all the things it is impossible to do with the object. When they do their presentations, their ideas are challenged by the other teams.
2. This can lead on to a discussion about how reversing the question can be a productive way to generate ideas or at least determine what is impossible. Also, there can be a further discussion on the use of technology or advancing technology to solve the problem.

65   Metamorphic Links
(Life's like that!)

Description   The participants develop their metaphor for the meaning of life.

Purpose   This shows the power of the metaphor in creative problem solving.

Materials   A pencil for each participant.
Paper for each participant.

Duration   10 minutes.

Procedure   Ask each participant to write down a metaphor for life. The following is one example. 'Life is like a tin of sardines. If you do find the key, it is still difficult to open. If you don't find the key it can be very messy. Even when you have opened it there is always something there that you can never get out of it.'

Review   Lead a discussion on the role of the metaphor in assisting soft thinking.

Variations   Be creative – think of your own!

66 Problem Sketch

Description A problem is drawn as a picture. *History:* This exercise is based on some of the soft systems approaches of the late 1980s. I have used it to free up problem definitions when they are described textually.

Purpose This exercise demonstrates alternative methods of looking at problems. Participants should use it as an opportunity to be as creative or 'off the wall' as they like.

Materials A pencil and paper for each team (or, preferably, marker pens and a flip chart).

Duration 70 minutes for two teams.

Procedure
1. Divide the participants into teams. (This exercise can be done individually or in teams. Teams usually generate the best results.)
2. Describe a problem.
3. Ask each team to draw a picture of the problem as it sees it. Allow 20 minutes for this stage.
4. Each team presents drawing to the group and discusses it. This should take 5 minutes.
5. Each team takes 20 minutes to draw a picture of what a solution to the problem might look like.
6. The teams present their solutions to the group and discuss them. Allow 10 minutes for this.

Review Discuss how the picture was created. Were there any fresh insights? Talk about the use of the right hand side of the brain as opposed to the left hand side.

Variation The teams draw a cartoon sequence to describe the problem.

VII

Closing

It is important to spend time closing at the end of an event, particularly if it has lasted a few days and participants have had to work closely together. I always allow time for participants to say goodbye both to the members of their own team and to the whole group. If participants have been away for a number of days it is worth reminding them to take care when driving and as they re-enter home life.

I remember being told by a lecturer in human behaviour of the time he attended a course on sensitivity. It was an excellent course. He rushed home to tell his wife all about it, and as soon as he arrived home he started to share the experiences with her. It was over coffee, at the end of the meal that she had lovingly prepared for him, that she finally stopped him in his tracks by saying 'and you didn't learn a thing!' – very sensitive?

During the closing session there may also be an opportunity to run some exercises that can produce useful feedback about the event.

My personal favourite of the exercises in this chapter is **Memories**, which was introduced by Ioan Tenner on one of my first courses.

67   Action Aides

Description   Team members assist each other in planning their next steps after the event.

Purpose   This exercise gives participants viable action planning support, and help in maintaining the team network after the event.

Materials   A flip chart and a pen for each team.
A pen for each participant.
Paper for each participant.

Duration   About 1 hour, for a team of 4.

Procedure
1. Each team member takes 5 minutes to decide on a key goal that he or she wishes to achieve during the next year. These are usually learning or business goals, but they can be personal, for example losing 25 lb (or 10 kg) of weight. The participant writes down his or her goal and name on a piece of paper.
2. The goals are then displayed for the rest of the team to see. If some of the goals are very similar they should be grouped together.
3. The team decides on the order in which the goals are going to be examined. Similar goals may be examined at the same time.
4. A member of the team writes a goal and the name of the person who owns the goal at the top of the flip chart. Below the goal, the member writes 'WHY?'. The person who owns this goal then states why he or she wishes to achieve it. Other members of the team may ask for clarification and discuss the reasoning. The reason is then written on the flip chart.
5. Next, 'WHEN' is written, and agreement is reached on when the goal is to be achieved.
6. 'HOW' is then written on the flip chart. This is the difficult question. The team helps the goal owner to draw up an action plan, or list the steps required to achieve the goal. Remember that 'by the inch it's a cinch, by the yard it's hard'. When the necessary steps have been determined, the team decides which of its members can help the goal owner to take each step. Against each step, 'WHO' is written, together with the name of the person who will help and when the step will be achieved. It may be necessary to review the end date for the plan in the light of the intermediate steps. Once the plan has been agreed, it is signed by all the team members.
7. The team then moves on to the next goal. If there are a number of similar action plans, these should be considered at the same time.

8. The process continues until all the members of the team have action plans.

Review   None.

Variations   None.

68   Air Mail

Description   Statements and suggestions about the event are written on sheets of paper. Each of these is folded up to make an aeroplane and flown towards the leaders of the course.

Purpose   This a fun approach to generating closing off feedback.

Materials   A pen for each participant.
A sheet of A4 (or letter size) paper for each participant.

Duration   5 minutes.

Procedure
1. The participants write down their feedback on sheets of A4 paper. The feedback can consist of statements about the event and/or suggestions for future events.
2. Each participant folds his or her piece of paper into a paper aeroplane.
3. When all the aeroplanes are ready, on the word 'fly', they are flown towards the course leaders at the front of the room.
4. As soon as the paper aeroplanes are flying the delegates begin saying their farewells. When the farewells are over and the participants have left the room, the leaders collect up the air mail.

Review   None.

Variations   None.

69   Cascading Handshake

Description   Each participant progressively shakes the hands of all the others and wishes them well in the future.

Purpose   This is a closing off exercise that can be great fun as the handshakes progress.

Materials   None.

Duration   A few minutes, depending on the size of the group.

Procedure
1. The participants stand in a line.
2. The leaders, at each end of the line, turn to their immediate neighbours, and shake hands with them. They make a positive statement during the handshake.
3. Each leader then moves on to the next person in the line and shakes his or her hand.
4. The people who first had their hands shaken by the leaders follow behind the leaders to shake hands with their immediate neighbours.
5. This process continues until the two handshaking lines meet. They will probably be side by side at right angles to the original lines. The leaders then shake each other's hands, and progress along each other's lines followed by their neighbours, as before, until everybody has shaken everybody else's hand.
6. This exercise can become somewhat chaotic at the end, but there will be laughter as everybody tries to ensure that no-one is missed.

Review   None.

Variation   This exercise can be used as an ice breaker in which names are exchanged during the handshake. It is, however, unlikely that many names will be remembered.

70   Commercial Break

Description   This is a creative review for the last evening of a course. Each team produces a 60 second TV commercial for the course.

Purpose   Three threads run through this exercise: team creativity, a review of the key points of the course, and a recognition that the closing process has begun.

Materials   None.

Duration   The preparation is done in the evening, and the teams can take as long as they need. The presentation of four advertisements should take 10 minutes.

Procedure
1. Explain that the exercise is a creative review covering the week. Each team has to prepare a 1 minute commercial for the course. The commercial must follow the advertisers' code of practice, that is, it must be honest, decent and legal.
2. The teams draw lots to determine the order of the next day's presentations.
3. The teams have the evening in which to prepare their commercials.
4. The next morning, the teams present their commercials.

Review   None. However, listen carefully to the commercials. There will be a number of pointers about the course.

Variations   None.

71   I'm OK, You're OK

Description   This is a paired closing off exchange.

Purpose   This exercise reinforces interviews prior to event closing.

Materials   None.

Duration   15–20 minutes, depending on the size of the group.

Procedure
1. The participants are paired off. If there is an odd number in the group, there will always be one spare person during each exchange.
2. Each pair decides who will speak. This person begins by saying 'I'm OK because ...' and then something positive and true about the event which has helped him or her. The person then says 'and you're OK because ...' and then something true and positive about the event and his or her partner. The roles are then reversed.
3. When both partners have spoken, then each finds a new partner to speak to. The exercise is repeated until everybody in the group has spoken to everyone else.

Review   None.

Variations   None.

72   Memories

Description   Participants write down their main memories, learnings, ideas etc. for the event on cards, and these are displayed for all the other participants to see.

Purpose   This exercise visually closes the event, which needs to have lasted for four or more days.

Materials   You need plenty of cards and plastic re-usable adhesive, or large Post-its® or similar repositional notes. You also need a marker pen for each participant.

Duration   10 minutes.

Procedure   1.   Place a pile of cards or Post-its® in the middle of the room. Ask the participants to pick up some cards or Post-its® and write or draw pictures of some of the memories they will be taking away from the event.

2.   The participants then stick their cards or Post-its® on a wall. (You can use an existing wall or create a wall from pinboards etc.)

3.   Everybody gathers round and looks at the memories. *Note:* This can be a very moving time for people who have worked closely together over a few days. Allow time for them to talk amongst themselves as they look at the wall.

Review   None. Close the event.

Variations None.

73 Spotlight

Description   All the participants have 30 seconds to give their views of the course. This exercise is based on the game of pass the parcel. Music is played, and a torch or any other object that can act as the 'speaker's badge' is passed round to music. When the music stops, the person with the torch is in the 'spotlight'. He or she has 30 seconds to make true and positive statements about the event. When the music starts again the torch is passed round again.

Purpose   This exercise allows delegates to comment on the event and make supportive statements about each other.

Materials   A tape recorder.
A watch.
A torch.

Duration   About 15–20 minutes for 20 people.

Procedure   1.   Explain that this exercise is the start of the closing down phase of the event. Sit the participants in a circle and explain the rules.
2.   Hand the torch to one person in the circle. Start the music. The torch is passed round the circle clockwise.
3.   Without looking at the group, stop the exercise after a few seconds. Whoever is holding the torch speaks about the course for 30 seconds.
4.   After 30 seconds, start the music again and repeat the process.
5.   If the person who is left holding the torch when the music stops has already spoken, the torch is passed on to the next person who has not spoken. This person will have less time to speak because the timing starts as soon as the music stops.
6.   The exercise continues until everybody has spoken.

Review   None.

Variations   None.

74   Talk To the Animals

Description   The participants talk about the course to a toy animal sitting in the middle of the group.

Purpose   This is a non-threatening way to elicit comments about the event. It is particularly useful if there has been some acrimony amongst participants, or if they are unlikely to say anything constructive if the process is facilitated by a course leader.

Materials   You need a teddy bear or a similar animal. Use an animal that is perceived as caring, for example a rabbit or a badger. Do not use snakes, sharks or dragons. You will also need a camcorder.

Duration   10 minutes maximum.

Procedure   1.   Set up the animal at the front of the group of participants and focus the camcorder on it. Explain to the participants that the animal is going to conduct a group review, and that it is being videotaped to capture their comments.

            2.   All the comments, which should be true and stated in a positive spirit, must be addressed to the chair. The participant should start

by saying 'Teddy' [or whatever animal is in the chair (it may have a name)], 'I wish to say that ...'. You should start the exercise off so that participants understand the procedure.

3. Continue the exercise for 10 minutes, or finish it earlier if the comments start to dry up.

Review   None.

Variations None.

75   Words of Appreciation

Description   Each team member writes three true and positive statements about the other members of the team.

Purpose   This is a team closing exercise in which the members of the team have the opportunity to show how much they have appreciated the others during the event. It will only work if a team has been working closely together for a number of days during an event. Typically, the team will have seven or fewer members.

Materials   Enough A5 paper or cards for every team member to write a note to every other team member.
A pen for every participant.

Duration   Allow 1 hour. I have known some teams that wanted to spend a great deal of time closing off.

Procedure   1. Hand each team member sufficient materials to send all the others a note. On the front of each note, the participant should write 'To X' (the person to whom the comments are addressed), and 'From Y' (his or her own name). On the other side, the sender should write three true and positive comments about the addressee.
2. Each team member should write a note to all the other team members.
3. When all the notes have been written, they should be handed to the addressees.
4. The recipients should then spend some time reading the comments.

Review   None.

Variation   The participants can also send a note to themselves.

Beginnings and Endings

Michèle Barca and Kate Cobb

An indispensable collection of 40 icebreakers and 30 closing exercises. Each short icebreaking exercise is an ideal motivator, puts the group at ease and breaks down inhibitions.

The closing exercises enable you to 'finish off' your training session and allows participants to reflect positively upon what they have learnt.

The exercises are ready-to-run and have step-by-step instructions. You can use them in any training session regardless of subject or group competence.

1993   164 pages   1 85904 037 3

Gower

Designing Training Programmes

Dick Leatherman

You've carried out a training needs analysis and listed the topics your programme should cover. Now how do you set about determining the content? Or identifying the most appropriate teaching methods?

Dick Leatherman's book sets out a ten-step process for developing training programmes tailored to your own requirements. Based on a coherent set of learning principles, it guides you through each of the activities involved, from formulating objectives to designing the post-course evaluation. Additional sections provide expert advice on reviewing off-the-shelf training packages and choosing, and working with, outside consultants.

For trainers and others seeking a simple, systematic approach to the design of programmes Dr Leatherman's book would be hard to better.

1996   144 pages   0 566 07770 1

Handbook of Management Games

5th Edition

Chris Elgood

This is the fifth edition of what is, quite simply, the most comprehensive reference to management games available, covering everything from how to run them to how to obtain them. The book explains what management games are, how the types differ from each other and how they compare with other methods of promoting learning. It offers a rationale for their use and confronts the difficulties of nomenclature that exist and the relationship between different views of the learning process. Also examined is the relationship between enjoyment and learning.

The directory section has descriptions of about 300 currently available management games, classified in various ways. Administrative details such as the number of players, the number of teams and the time required are provided, together with information on target group, subject areas, nature and purpose.

1993   352 pages   0 566 07306 4

Gower

Icebreakers

Edited by Andy Kirby

Are you looking for ways to begin your training with a bang? Would you like to liven up those sluggish after lunch-sessions? Could you use a new approach to start-of-course introductions? Then Andy Kirby's collection of games is for you.

From 'Animal Crackers' to 'Yukkies', by way of 'Creeping Death', 'Fruit and Spoon Race', 'If I Were Famous' and 'Walking the Plank', the seventy-five games in this volume are guaranteed to enrich any trainer's repertoire. Compiled by a team of five trainers with a wide variety of experience between them, they represent a rich mixture of styles and treatments. There are also an index of objectives to help you choose the most appropriate event, photocopiable masters of all participants' material, and an introduction explaining how you can derive the maximum benefit from the book.

Icebreakers is one of the most useful and versatile training resources available.

1993   136 pages   1 85904 044 6

Gower

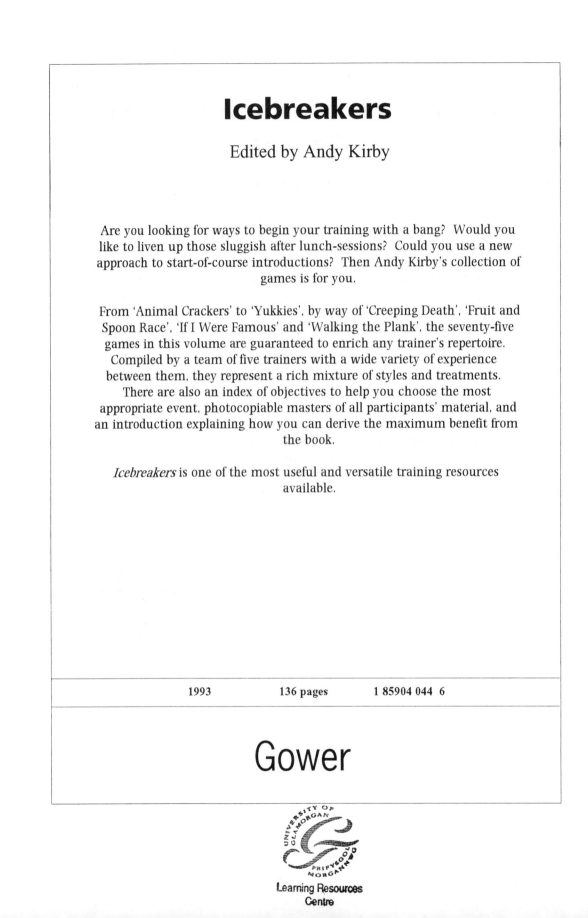

Learning Resources
Centre